BLESSED
IN THE
MESS

STUDY GUIDE

BLESSED
IN THE
MESS

STUDY GUIDE

HOW TO EXPERIENCE
GOD'S GOODNESS
IN THE MIDST OF LIFE'S PAIN

JOYCE MEYER

FaithWords

NEW YORK • NASHVILLE

FaithWords
Hachette Book Group
1290 Avenue of the Americas, New York, NY 10104
faithwords.com
twitter.com/faithwords

First Edition: September 2023

FaithWords is a division of Hachette Book Group, Inc. The FaithWords name and logo are trademarks of Hachette Book Group, Inc.

The publisher is not responsible for websites (or their content) that are not owned by the publisher.

The Hachette Speakers Bureau provides a wide range of authors for speaking events. To find out more, go to hachettespeakersbureau.com or email HachetteSpeakers@hbgusa.com.

FaithWords books may be purchased in bulk for business, educational, or promotional use. For information, please contact your local bookseller or the Hachette Book Group Special Markets Department at special.markets@hbgusa.com.

ISBNs: 978-1-5460-4693-6 (trade paperback)

Printed in the United States of America

LSC-C

Printing 1, 2023

CONTENTS

INTRODUCTION

If you've lived long at all, you know that life isn't always easy. Thankfully, we do experience good times, but we also have our share of pain and difficulty. God does not promise us a trouble-free existence. In fact, His Word teaches us to expect the opposite. Jesus says in John 16:33, "In the world you will have tribulation; but be of good cheer, I have overcome the world" (NKJV). In addition to this clear warning that we will certainly face troubles, the Bible is filled with instructions on how to handle ourselves when difficulty does come our way.

I refer to the hurts we deal with and the problems people face as our "messes." I often hear people say, "My life is a mess," or "This situation is a mess." What they mean is that life has become difficult, painful, or confusing. As Jesus promised, no one is immune to trials and tribulations.

The good news is that we can be blessed in the midst of our mess. We don't have to wait for things to get better. Right in the middle of our pain, in our most discouraging moments, when situations seem to be at their worst, we can experience God's goodness and His blessings.

This study guide, which accompanies the book *Blessed in the Mess*, is designed to help you apply the lessons of the book to your individual circumstances and your personal life. I have lived through many messes, starting when I was just a child. And I have seen God's faithfulness, received His blessings, and experienced His redemption in every situation.

My prayer for you in the midst of whatever mess you are going through is that *Blessed in the Mess* and this companion study guide will help you navigate the pain and problems in your life in such a way that God's blessings and the good things He does in you and through you as you walk through your trials will far outweigh the negatives of your situation.

Keep praying, keep hoping, remain positive, be patient, and stay close to God, and you'll be blessed in the midst of your mess.

BLESSED
IN THE
MESS

STUDY GUIDE

PART 1

God Can Bless Your Mess

CHAPTER 1
The Double Blessing

1. When you think about your "mess," meaning the pain you feel right now or the problems you are facing, what situation comes to mind?
2. I am thankful that God has allowed the story of my mess—sexual abuse as a child and other difficulties—to help other people. What is your story?
3. How do you think your story could help other people?
4. When people intend to hurt us or cause us trouble, God can use it for good (Genesis 50:20). How have you seen Him do this in your life or in a situation involving someone around you?
5. In my story, I shared about how I felt abandoned because my mother and other relatives did not take action when I needed their help. Read Psalm 82:3 and Proverbs 31:8. What does the Bible teach us as believers to do in situations like this?

God Comes on the Scene

1. Take a moment to think about your salvation experience. What were the circumstances?
2. How has your personal relationship with God through Jesus Christ made a difference in your life?

3. At what point in your life did you first begin to sense God drawing you to Him? Were you very young, or did it happen later? How did He make Himself known to you and begin to draw your heart toward Him?

4. Before you received Jesus as your Lord and Savior, did you see yourself as a sinner? If so, what made you realize that?

5. Perhaps you have noticed the effects or consequences of sin in your life or in someone else's. What are some examples of this?

6. Have there been difficult situations in your life that God didn't get you out of right away? How has your walk with God grown closer as a result of the suffering you've endured?

7. According to Hebrews 5:8–9, what did suffering accomplish in the life of Jesus?

8. How can your suffering equip you to help someone else?

9. Do you ever keep people at a distance due to fear of getting hurt? After reading that we need other people and we aren't created to be alone, what are some things you can do to be more available and engaged in relationships?

10. How could you help people around you who struggle to connect in relationships and tend to keep others at a distance?

11. Why does deciding not to need other people not work?

God Changes People's Hearts

1. Have you ever made mistakes similar to the ones Hannah made? What happened?

2. How has God changed your heart in this situation?

3. Why is jumping to conclusions about people before getting to know them or understanding their circumstances a mistake?

4. How could you better discern God's will about a relationship when you meet someone new? How would prayer and knowing God's Word help you do this?

5. What can you learn from Hannah's story? What were some signs in her thoughts and behavior that showed God had changed her heart?

6. Would you be willing to pray as Hannah did, that God's will be done, even if you dislike someone? Why or why not?

7. Do you feel there are any relationships in your life where a change of heart may be needed? Ask God to show you and help you make the adjustments you need to make.

A Bad Relationship That Never Improved

1. Think about the ways you have observed this statement to be true in your life or in a situation you have observed and describe them: "Desperate people do not make good decisions."

2. Consider Isaiah 45:3. How has God given you treasures in darkness?

3. Can you see any signs of God's provision and His hand at work in my situation? What were they?

4. How does the story of my son David encourage you?

5. Have you or anyone you know made a bad decision out of desperation? What were the circumstances and results?

6. What are some ways to protect yourself from pursuing relationships with people who will likely have a negative influence on you?

Blessed after a Mess

1. Have you ever felt God calling you to do something that seemed impossible? How did you respond?

2. Do you sense God leading you to do something impossible right now? If so, how does my story encourage you?

3. God clearly worked in my life and developed my faith. How has He done this for you?

4. Why do you think that learning to be under authority before we accept positions of authority over others is important?

5. Have you ever lacked anything or desperately wanted something and later received it? How did the season of lack cause you to appreciate it more when you finally got it?

6. Is there anything you're still praying for and waiting to receive? How can my story encourage you as you wait?

7. Have you ever felt you lacked the background or skills to do something great for God? How does 1 Corinthians 1:26–31 encourage you?

8. Do you need an increased hunger and love for God's Word? Pray now and ask God for it. This is a prayer He loves to answer.

9. Have you ever felt you didn't know how to give or receive love? How can receiving God's love help you begin?

10. Romans 8:28 teaches us that "all things work together for good" in the lives of those who love God and are called according to His purpose (NKJV). How have the bad things that have happened to you worked together for good in your life?

11. Saint Augustine said, "Trials come to prove and improve us." How have you seen this statement ring true in your life or the lives of others?

The Promise That Changed My Life

1. What does it mean to receive a "double portion"? How does Isaiah 61:7 give you the hope of restoration for what you've suffered?

2. Ask God for a double portion by praying this prayer or a similar one in your own words: "God, please give me a double portion, along with joy, for the hurt and shame I suffered when _____."

3. Define what *recompense* means. How does this work hand in hand with God's justice?

4. Do you feel you are often waiting for the next bad thing to happen? How can you renew your mind according to God's Word and begin to live with the expectation that He will do good things for you?

5. Why is hope a powerful motivator? According to Proverbs 13:12, what can happen when people don't have hope?

6. Fill in the blanks in this sentence from the third paragraph of the section "The Promise That Changed My Life": "When we have hope, we live with the _____ that God will do something _____ for us."

7. Who can have hope?

8. One way to gain more hope is to believe and repeat this phrase several times a day: "Something good is going to happen to me because God is good." Try this for at least a week and notice how your attitude becomes more hopeful by the renewing of your mind (Romans 12:2).

9. Why was Job's prayer for his friends in Job 42:10 an important step for him to take before he received his double blessing?

10. How can unforgiveness block the blessings God wants to pour out in your life? Is there anyone you need to forgive and pray

for as you prepare to receive the blessing God has for you? Ask God to show you and help you do it.

11. In 2 Kings 2:1–12 Elisha asked for a double portion of Elijah's spirit, and God granted his request. In what area of your life do you want God to give you a double portion? Follow Elisha's example and ask God for it.

12. Proverbs 6:30–31 talks about the sevenfold blessing when something has been stolen. Has anything been taken from you that you can ask God to restore based on these verses?

13. Do you need to restore anything to anyone you've hurt or from whom you may have taken something? Ask God to lead you and give you strength to do what you need to do.

14. What did you learn from the story about the television station? Why is it important for us to release situations such as this one to God—even if they don't involve something like teaching God's Word on television? What can He accomplish through our obedience?

I Am Amazed

1. What did you learn from my story about God turning my mess into my message and ministry? How does this encourage you and give you hope that God can use your situation for good?

2. God has a way of turning a situation you think will be your worst enemy into your best friend. Can you see any ways He may be doing this in the midst of your mess right now? What are they?

3. Could you identify with Sawyer's story? How has God allowed you to comfort others because of what you have been through?

4. Sawyer could have kept walking when he saw his classmate crying, thinking his own life was too messed up to help anyone else. What step of faith did he take instead?

5. How do you think that step of faith and the others Sawyer has taken to comfort the people God has put in his path have helped him become the godly man he is today?

6. How could your mess become your message and your ministry? Are there people who could benefit from what you've learned? What examples can you think of?

7. The second-to-last paragraph of the section "I Am Amazed," which begins with "To experience blessing in the midst of your mess," lists several decisions and actions you will need to take to experience blessing in the midst of your mess. What are they?

8. How does Zechariah 9:12 give you hope that God can bless you?

Who Made This Mess?

1. Do you ever use or think of the word *trouble* to describe the pain, the mess, or the stress in your life? If you were to define the trouble or troubles you currently face, what would you say? In other words, what trouble or troubles are you dealing with right now?

2. According to the second paragraph of chapter 2, how does trouble test us? How have you experienced this in your life?

3. According to James 1:2–4, why should you be joyful when you encounter trouble or trials?

4. In what ways have you grown spiritually during hard times?

5. Do you ever blame others for your bad behavior? How can you overcome this, according to John 8:32?

6. In what situations have you found yourself not feeling like obeying God? How did you grow spiritually when you chose to do what was right in spite of the way you felt?

7. According to Romans 12:18, how are we to live in relationships with other people? When you think of a specific relationship that seems to be a mess right now, what can you do to remain peaceful with the other person?

8. Has the thought that you can do the right thing even when you don't want to ever occurred to you? Or have you tended to allow your desires to dictate your decisions? Will you make

a fresh commitment today to obey God, even if it seems hard and even if you don't want to?

9. How has Jesus set an example for us in obeying God even when doing so is difficult?

Blame Has Been Around a Long Time

1. What was the first occurrence of blame in the Bible? What were the consequences? What do you need to do to be free from these consequences in your life?

2. How can taking responsibility for your actions help you avoid the trap of sin and blame?

3. What did you learn from the story of Abram and Sarai? Think for a minute about how things could have turned out differently if they'd trusted God.

4. Even if someone else has caused you pain, why is it important to take responsibility for your own behavior?

5. Why does hiding or running from your problems not work to your benefit?

6. Have you ever blamed someone or something for a mess you have made? What were the circumstances? What were the consequences of placing blame instead of taking responsibility?

7. Are you guilty of placing blame instead of taking responsibility in the following areas? Check all that apply. Then, make a note about how you can begin to take responsibility for these situations with God's help.
   • ungodly behavior
   • being overweight
   • poor stewardship of finances or resources

8. Can you remember a time when you took responsibility for something you did or said, even if doing so was difficult, and the situation turned out better than you expected? What happened?

9. Take the advice in the last paragraph of the section "Blame Has Been Around a Long Time" and ask God if you have opened a door to a problem you are currently facing, meaning that you have played a role in allowing or creating the situation.

Where Have All the Responsible People Gone?

1. Fill in the blanks in this sentence from the first paragraph of the section "Where Have All the Responsible People Gone?": We cannot have _____ for ourselves or from others unless we take _____ for ourselves.

2. Have you ever *not* wanted to take responsibility for something that really was your responsibility and allowed someone else to do it? What were the results?

3. If you have children, how can you teach them to accept responsibility for their actions?

4. What does Romans 8:28 promise will happen if you take the first step in your recovery by taking responsibility for your actions?

5. When you realize you've made a bad decision, why are repentance and an apology better than guilt and condemnation?

Procrastination

1. What did you learn from the story from the Book of Haggai? What were the consequences of the people's procrastination?

2. Why is procrastination deceptive? Why does planning to obey God not equal obedience?

3. Is there something you know God wants you to do, but you've been procrastinating and haven't done it? Ask Him to help you to take a step of obedience today.

God Is a Rewarder

1. According to Hebrews 11:6, whom does God reward?

2. If you've made a mess of some sort, what are the three things you can do to be blessed in spite of it?

3. God is a rewarder, and His desire is to reward not to punish, but why does He sometimes need to correct us?

4. Why isn't it wrong to expect a reward for obeying God? What are some rewards you can expect from your obedience?

5. Why can't you simply assume that God's promises will automatically come to pass? What are three ways you can release your faith for the promises God has given you to be fulfilled?

6. Do you believe God will still bless you even if you've made a mess out of your life? What can you learn from the apostle Peter's example?

CHAPTER 3

Storms and Rainbows

1. Have you ever experienced, or are you currently in the middle of, any storms in your life? How has God helped you through them? How can you begin to look for a rainbow at the end?

2. In the middle of a storm, it's important not just to focus on the negative aspects of the situation but also to look for the positive ones. Can you identify any blessings in the midst of your storms?

3. In what ways was David blessed in the middle of his mess in Psalm 23?

4. When you're waiting for God to bless you in the midst of your mess, what is an important and necessary part of doing things God's way?

5. Do you find forgiving the people who have hurt you difficult? How can forgiving out of obedience to God empower you to forgive and set you free to experience His blessings?

6. Even though your enemies may not deserve forgiveness, what do you deserve? How can you give yourself this gift?

7. Fill in the blanks in this sentence from the fifth-to-last paragraph of the first section of chapter 3: "When you are _____ to someone who has really _____ you, it disarms the _____."

8. Do you have any friends like Job's who were not there for you when you needed them most? Take time to forgive and pray for them now.

9. Why is it true that "as long as we are bitter, we cannot get better"? Think of one person you feel bitter toward. What is one thing you can do today to bless that person?

10. How do Psalm 37:3 and Romans 12:21 help us to bless our enemies, even when it's the last thing we feel like doing?

Go Through

1. According to Hebrews 6:11, what are the two qualities we need to cultivate when we go through trials?

2. What did you learn from Daniel's example in the lions' den? As a Christian, has your faith ever been tested?

3. Have you ever been asked to do something unethical, immoral, or illegal? How did you handle it? If you did the right thing, did your example of walking by faith in God inspire anyone to want to know more about Christ? Even if you aren't aware of it, you may have been a good witness to someone.

4. Fill in the blanks in this sentence from the last paragraph of the section "Go Through": Always remember that if you do the _____ _____, even if you _____ _____ initially because of your decision, in the end you will get a_____ _____.

Refuse to Compromise

1. Have you ever come under fire for openly practicing your faith, as Daniel did when he prayed with the windows open? What happened?

2. Are you sometimes tempted to be quiet about your faith when there's a risk of persecution or suffering? How did God bless Shadrach, Meshach, and Abed-Nego for their obedience? How does their story encourage you to stand firm?

3. Nebuchadnezzar, a nonbeliever, believed in God after seeing the faith of His people. What opportunities do you have in your everyday life to demonstrate your faith in the presence of people who do not yet have a personal relationship with God through Jesus Christ?

4. Daniel 3:25 says the three men were "unbound and unharmed." Do you believe your obedience during difficult times could lead to your freedom from bondage? Pray that God would release you and set you free.

Facing My Fears for My Family

1. Was there anything you could identify with in Anne's story? Have you ever felt like a high-functioning trauma survivor making your way through life?

2. Anne's life looked pretty good on the surface, but how did her unresolved bitterness negatively affect her family?

3. What were the six things Anne did to position herself for God to set her free? What changed about her after that, and how did her transformation affect her daughters?

Paul and Silas in Prison

1. We know that many early believers were persecuted for preaching the gospel. But Paul and Silas were thrown into jail for another reason. What did they do to cause such offense?

2. Most people would be bitter and angry if they were beaten and thrown into prison, but how did Paul and Silas respond? How did their response affect the people around them, especially the jailer?

3. What were the four steps of obedience Paul and Silas displayed when going through this storm? What blessing came from this?

CHAPTER 4

Overcoming Tests, Trials, and Temptations

1. Why must you sometimes go through difficulties and messes personally in order to help other people?

2. How is dealing with difficulty like lifting weights in the gym? How does 1 Corinthians 10:13 encourage you?

3. What difficulties have you endured that made you stronger in your faith? In what ways have these experiences enabled you to help others?

4. Have you ever viewed your financial worries as tests from God to grow your faith? How would you grade yourself? Do you think you're passing or failing? If you feel you're failing this test repeatedly, what can you do to better trust in God's provision and start passing these tests?

5. How does knowing that your worth and value are not in what you do but in who you are in Christ give you peace about whatever God may call you to do?

6. John 17:9 and Romans 8:34 say that Jesus is praying for you when you experience tests, trials, and temptations. How will this knowledge help you go through them better?

7. What are the five things you need to do if the devil is trying to shake your faith? What can you expect if you do them?

Tests Come on the Road to Fulfilled Promises

1. Why do you think Abraham had to wait so long and experience many trials and tests of his faith before he saw the complete fulfillment of God's promise?

2. Have you been waiting a long time for God to do something in your life? How can Abraham's example encourage you?

3. Once you pass one of God's tests, does that mean you will never have to be tested that way again? Why or why not? How does the weight training example apply?

4. Fill in the blanks in this sentence from the last paragraph of the section "Tests Come on the Road to Fulfilled Promises": As we go through _____, we have _____ they will eventually _____ and that we will be _____ _____ when we get to the other side of them.

From Test to Testimony

1. What does it mean for your test to become your testimony? Do you have any examples of this in your own life? Why do you think it is an effective way to share your faith?

2. If you had to write a short paragraph about how God has made a specific test into a testimony for you, what would you say?

3. Why is it that some people don't have a testimony of victory regarding their trials? What did they fail to do?

4. God does not rejoice in our sufferings. According to the last paragraph of the section "From Test to Testimony," what does cause Him to rejoice when we go through suffering?

Suffering

1. The world is full of suffering. In what ways do you see people suffering around you?

2. Romans 5:3–4 says suffering produces three positive attributes. What are they? Give examples of the ways your suffering has developed your faith in one or more of these areas.

3. What are some examples of "milk" messages that infants in Christ love to hear? Why are they important to new believers?

4. What are some examples of "solid food" messages that spiritually growing Christians need to hear? Why are they important to our journey of maturity as believers?

5. I suffered in the flesh as I learned to submit to my husband's authority according to Ephesians 5:22–24. In what ways have you had to endure suffering in order to be obedient to God's Word and grow spiritually?

6. What does it mean to "put to death" what belongs to your earthly nature (Colossians 3:5)? Why is this necessary to live a victorious Christian life?

7. What happens when we give in to the desires of our flesh? What happens when we deprive them of the power to rule us? Remember, what we feed will grow, and what we don't feed, starves.

8. Has someone ever mistreated you, and you really wanted to confront them? What do Romans 12:18 and Colossians 3:15 say you should do instead?

No Parking in Your Pain

1. What is the biggest reason some people are "parked in their pain"? If this describes you, what is the one thing you can do

today to move past your pain? Do this now, and ask God to heal your brokenness and wounds.

2. According to Psalm 37:1–3, what will happen to those who do evil in the world? How can this knowledge help you to stop trying to punish the people who have hurt you and get your own justice?

3. What does this statement mean: "Life is not fair, but God is just"? How have you seen this to be true in your life or in a situation you are familiar with?

4. Fill in the blanks in this phrase from the first sentence of the last paragraph of the section "No Parking in Your Pain": God doesn't ask us to _____; He asks us to _____ Him.

PART 2

Living a Blessed Life

CHAPTER 5

Choose to Be Blessed

1. When God created human beings, He never wanted our lives to become a mess. What happened in Genesis 3 to open the door to the sin, suffering, pain, and wrongdoing that happens in the world?

2. According to Ephesians 1:7, why did Jesus come? Do you believe the blessed way of life that God originally intended for us is still available? What do we need to do to experience it?

3. What do these scriptures teach you about the blessed life?
   • Deuteronomy 28:3–6
   • 2 Corinthians 9:8
   • Ephesians 1:3

4. Are your friends helping you grow in godliness? Do they encourage you in your faith?

5. What are the three types of people in Psalm 1:1 you should avoid spending time with and taking advice from? Why is staying in relationship with them not a good idea?

6. What does the Bible say about consulting fortune tellers, mediums, or psychics or practicing astrology? Why is it important to stay away from these things if you want God to bless you?

Choose Your Friends Wisely

1. Have you ever had a close friend who was a bad influence on you? What were the signs, and what did you do about it?

2. If you are currently in a relationship with a person or a group of people who are not a good influence on you, what steps can you take to distance yourself from them?

3. Do you know any mockers? What are their characteristics? What negative effects have you or others experienced as a result of their behavior?

4. What is the difference between committing sin occasionally or accidentally and living a lifestyle of intentional, habitual sin?

5. Are you acquainted with any gossips? How has their "talebearing" affected you and other relationships in your life? How do you plan to limit their influence on you?

6. If you want to be a witness for God, you can't distance yourself completely from nonbelievers. How can you ensure you are affecting them instead of allowing them to infect you?

7. Why is it so important to spend time studying, listening to, and reading God's Word?

8. What are the three characteristics of a godly person mentioned in Psalm 1:3? How many of your friends exhibit these qualities? If you don't have friends like this, ask God to lead you to some.

9. What does it mean to prosper? And how does *prosperity* refer to more than just money?

10. What instructions does Joshua 1:8 say to follow to become prosperous?

11. What protects us from becoming greedy?

12. Fill in the blanks in this sentence from the second-to-last paragraph of the section "Choose Your Friends Wisely":

Having _____ is good, as long as _____ doesn't have us.

13. What is the first and most important key to living a blessed life?

14. In what practical ways can you put God first in your life?

Obedience Leads to Blessing

1. How has God blessed you when you were obedient to Him? If there were times when you didn't obey Him, what were the consequences?

2. Has there been anyone who has helped you to stay on the "narrow path" and off the "broad path"? How did they help you?

3. Why does what you do prove what you believe?

4. How does anger give Satan an open door to work in your life? What are some practical steps you can take to not let the sun go down on your anger? Are you angry with anyone right now? Close the door to the enemy by choosing to forgive them.

5. Why does Jesus command us to forgive? In what ways does unforgiveness forfeit the blessed life He died for you to have?

6. What is your biggest challenge when trying to forgive? In the section "Obedience Leads to Blessing," I shared eight things to consider when you find it difficult to forgive. Which one was most helpful to you? Think of someone you have trouble forgiving. Could you put this into practice today to forgive them?

Obey God, Not People

1. According to Acts 5:29, why can't you be a people-pleaser and a God-pleaser at the same time? Have you ever tried to do this? What happened?

2. What does obedience require?

3. Fill in the blanks in this sentence from the last paragraph of the section "Obey God, Not People": "Even those of us who truly _____ to _____ God will _____ _____, and we thank God for His _____."

4. How do Romans 8:1 and Lamentations 3:22–23 give you hope that when you make a mistake you don't have to waste time feeling guilty?

Freedom from Selfishness

1. What does Jesus say is necessary for us to be His disciples, based on Matthew 16:24–25?

2. Max Lucado says, "God loves us too much to indulge our every whim." What does this mean?

3. If you live your life as though everything is about you, what will you be left with?

4. Explain this statement: "To be set free from self is truly the greatest freedom we can have." Why is this true?

5. On a scale of 1–10, with 1 being not good at all and 10 being great, how would you rate yourself in terms of being able to remain content and happy when you do not get your way?

6. How has following God given you more contentment, even when you've had to sacrifice to obey Him?

7. Are you settling for a life that is less than blessed? If so, how can you begin to change that?

8. Do you believe that to be a Christian you must be miserable and have nothing? Because God's Word doesn't support this, how can you renew your mind in this area?

9. Part of being faithful over what God has given us is to be generous in giving to others. How can you grow in generosity as God continues to bless you?

10. What are you doing to help the poor? Are you giving financially to organizations that serve them? Do you contribute to a local food bank or clothing ministry? How might you do more to help people in need?

CHAPTER 6

Don't Be Offended by Trouble

1. In the parable of the farmer, found in Mark 4:3–20, who does the farmer represent? What does the seed symbolize? What does the ground represent?
2. Have you ever sown spiritual seed by sharing God's Word about Jesus with someone, only to see it "blown away" by some device of Satan? What happened to take away the message?
3. How has the enemy prevented you from reading God's Word? What type of distractions get in the way?
4. Was there ever a time when you had rocky ground in your heart when it comes to God's Word? What were you thinking or feeling at that time? How does this help you understand people who easily fall away from God's teaching?
5. How do people with inflated egos often respond when they face trouble?
6. The English word *offense* comes from the Greek word *skandalon*. What does *skandalon* mean, and how does it help us understand offenses?
7. Why does Satan use offense as a way to trap people, and why is it so dangerous to a person's walk with God? How do you escape the enemy's snare when he tries to bait you with bitterness, resentment, or unforgiveness?

8. What does James 1:19–20 (AMPC) teach us about dealing with offense?

9. Why is Jesus a rock of salvation to a believer but a rock of offense to a nonbeliever?

10. Do you know people for whom Jesus is a stumbling block because something bad happened to them? What could you say to someone in this situation to help them see God's goodness?

11. Have you ever been offended by God because of something you didn't understand? How can Romans 8:28 and 11:33 help you trust Him more in the midst of unanswered questions?

12. How do you react when you face trouble or difficulty? Do you become angry with God, or do you trust Him? Ask God to give you the discernment to recognize Satan's schemes and the strength to avoid becoming offended.

13. Near the end of the first section of chapter 6, there are some questions about how you handle trouble. Here's your chance to answer them.
    • What is the attitude of your heart when you face difficulty?
    • Do you become angry with God, or do you trust Him?
    • Are you offended when you have trials and tribulations, or do you realize they are part of life and everyone has to deal with them?

14. Trials can affect us in at least two ways. What are they?

Putting Down Roots

1. Mark 4:17 says that those who fall away during times of trouble and persecution have no roots. When it comes to your faith, would you consider yourself a deeply rooted oak tree or a

shallow-rooted sapling? What can you do to grow deeper roots to withstand the storms of life?

2. According to Deuteronomy 8:2-3, why did God lead the Israelites through the wilderness for forty years? What kind of provision did He make for them during their long journey?

3. Have there been times in your life when you had to trust God day by day, as the Israelites had to trust Him for manna? How did these experiences help increase your trust in God?

4. On a scale of 1–10, with 1 being hardly at all and 10 being almost completely, how much do you trust God one day at a time? If needed, how can you grow in this area?

5. What process did the Israelites repeat throughout their years in the wilderness? If you are tempted to behave in a similar way, how can you resist the temptation?

6. How long should the Israelites' journey through the wilderness have taken? Why did God allow it to take forty years?

7. What did you learn from the example of the Israelites, who complained and grumbled when they encountered hardships and then couldn't enter the Promised Land?

8. Explain why this statement is true: The shortest, easiest way through a situation is not always the best way.

9. Has God taken you through any trials to strengthen your roots? What were they, and how did they make you stronger?

10. What does 1 Peter 5:8–9 say you should do to protect yourself from the devil? Does it encourage you to know that other believers are going through trials too? Take a minute to pray for those who are suffering right now.

11. First Peter 5:10 says God will allow you to suffer for a little while before He makes you what you ought to be. Have you ever exhausted yourself trying to get out of a trial or fix a problem,

only to give up and later give God the glory for helping you? How did He change you through this?

12. What is the difference between the works of the flesh and the works of God? Why do works of the flesh rarely succeed?

13. According to 1 Thessalonians 5:16–18, what is God's will for us in Christ Jesus?

Emotional Hearers

1. What is the definition of an emotional hearer?

2. What happens when we allow our emotions to rule us?

3. According to Psalm 94:12–13 (AMPC), why are we blessed when God disciplines and instructs us?

4. What is the key to not allowing ourselves to become upset?

5. Have you been circling a mountain a long time without a lot of progress? What do you need to do to get out of the wilderness?

6. How does God want us to be led? What will the Holy Spirit lead us to do and not to do?

7. Why can emotions be the believer's number one enemy? Why is it wise to talk less when trouble comes and emotions are running high?

8. Have you ever felt that as a believer you shouldn't have to suffer? How can this false view derail your faith?

9. Fill in the blanks in this sentence from the last paragraph of the section "Emotional Hearers": When _____ comes your way, don't let it _____ you.

CHAPTER 7

Be Careful What You Say

1. The opening quote for chapter 7 says, "Don't mix bad words with your bad mood." Have you ever done this? What happened?

2. Has your mouth ever gotten you in trouble? What emotions did you feel strongly when this happened?

3. Do you know anyone who speaks whatever comes into their mind? How has this affected their relationships?

4. Fill in the blanks in Proverbs 18:21 (AMP): "_____ and _____ are in the power of the _____, and those who love it and indulge it will eat its fruit and bear the consequences of their _____."

5. When have you brought life to someone by your words? When have you brought death? And when have you suffered the consequences of your words?

6. According to Proverbs 13:3, why should you be very careful about the words you speak?

7. What kinds of words do you usually speak when trouble comes? Commit to watch your words today. Try to replace every negative statement with a positive, faith-filled one based on God's Word using the formula from the book: "I'm [state how you feel], but [state a promise that applies from God's Word]."

8. How have other people's words affected you negatively?

9. Has anyone said or written to you something that affected you in positive ways?

10. How can you use your words to bless someone today?

Speak to the Mountain

1. Look at the list of Scripture-based examples of ways to speak to your problems. Which one or ones do you need to speak to a situation today? How do you think this will increase your faith?

2. Fill in the blanks in this sentence from the section "Speak to the Mountain": "As you speak positive words filled with _____, you will be _____ and _____."

3. According to Mark 11:25, what is the one thing you need to do before you speak God's Word to your problems?

4. After you have taken care of any unforgiveness in your heart, you have spoken God's Word to your troubles, you've prayed, and you believe that what you have asked for will be yours, what's the only thing left to do?

5. Write down on a sheet of paper the words of 1 John 5:14–15 (NKJV).

Who Is Religious?

1. What effect do "religious" people who don't discipline their tongues have on your faith? Have you ever been turned off by a church or group, or even faith in Jesus, by this?

2. How did the Pharisees act?

3. According to John 10:10, what is God's desire for you?

4. Based on 1 Peter 3:10, what should you do if you want to love life and see good days?

5. Have you ever acted like a Pharisee in your treatment of others? How could Ephesians 4:29–30 help set you free from this?

Goodness and Mercy Follow Us

1. What are the five blessings Psalm 23 says you can have in the midst of your troubles?

    1. "I will _____ no _____, for _____ are with _____" (v. 4).
    2. "You _____ a _____ before me in the _____ of my _____" (v. 5).
    3. "You _____ my _____ with _____" (v. 5).
    4. "My cup _____" (v. 5).
    5. "Surely _____ _____ and _____ will _____ me all the days of my life" (v. 6).

2. Can you remember a time when you were blessed while going through a difficult situation? What happened?

3. What does David mean when he says, "My cup overflows"? Have you experienced this?

4. Has God ever done good things for you while your enemies watched? What were the circumstances?

5. Commit today to speak and pray more like the psalmists, who spoke openly about their troubles but ended their psalms by declaring their trust in God and their expectation of His blessing. How can you do this in a specific situation you are facing right now?

6. What does it mean to walk by faith and talk by faith? Ask God to help you speak blessings over yourself and your loved ones daily.

Ask for God's Help

1. According to James 3:8, why do we need God's help to "tame the tongue"?
2. Have you ever wished you could take back something you had said to someone? I encourage you to get in the habit of praying in the spirit of Psalm 141:3 daily: "God, put a guard over my mouth, so I won't sin against You with my words."
3. Fill in the blanks in Proverbs 16:24 (NLT): "Kind _____ are like honey—_____ to the soul and _____ for the body."
4. According to Proverbs 12:18, what does "the tongue of the wise" bring?
5. Listen to the words other people speak this week. How do you think their words may have contributed to the state of their lives in positive ways or in negative ways?

How Jesus Handled His Temptation

1. What are the three physical conditions that can make you especially vulnerable to the devil's attacks?
2. In what ways have people tried to use Scripture against you? Have you ever felt the need to prove how "Christian" you are in response? Ask God to help you to be confident of who you are in Christ, free from the need to impress others.

3. Reflect on a time when you were tempted to compromise your faith to have something the world offered. Looking back, can you identify the temptation?

4. According to Luke 4:13, when will the devil stop attacking you? What can you do to better protect yourself from his lies?

5. Do you believe that after the testing comes the blessing? When have you experienced this?

CHAPTER 8

Understand the Power of a Good Attitude

1. In what ways does your attitude determine your altitude?

2. If your thought life were turned inside out for everyone around to see, what would it look like? Would you be proud or ashamed?

3. Have you ever worked with someone who was highly skilled but had a bad attitude? How did it affect your work environment?

4. What makes up for a lack of aptitude?

5. What can you learn from Jesus' example of humility? What was His reward?

6. What are some signs of a humble attitude?

7. Fill in the blanks in this sentence from the third-to-last paragraph of the first section of chapter 8: "No situation in life brings out our _____ _____ like _____ and _____ do."

8. Why is going through the tests God allows in our lives good for us?

9. What have you learned about yourself through the tests God has allowed in your life? What strengths have they developed in you?

10. What two qualities do trials develop in us?

11. What is an immature Christian's first response to trouble? Why is it important to grow past this toward patience and perseverance?

Take an Attitude Inventory

1. On a scale of 1–10, with 1 being very negative and 10 being extremely positive and thankful, how would you rate the attitude you typically have when you face trouble or problems?
2. What does keeping a good attitude require?
3. Why does God convict us of problem areas in our lives?
4. What are the two ways to think about trouble when it comes? What did you learn from the example of my fall?
5. Think about a difficulty you're currently experiencing. List some ways the problem could be worse, then thank God it isn't. The next time you have a problem, try this exercise.

Misery Is an Option

1. Have you ever considered that being miserable is a choice and that you're not stuck with the temperament you were born with? If you're in a bad mood, how can you change it?
2. Your attitude needs constant attention to keep it going in the right direction. What does Ephesians 4:23 say you should do?
3. Some people seem to be born with a good, positive attitude. On a scale of 1–10, with 1 being "I was born negative" and 10 being "I've been optimistic since I came out of the womb," how would you describe yourself?
4. In the midst of a negative situation you are currently facing, what steps can you take to become more positive?

How to Be Happy

1. What is the key to avoiding misery in the midst of trials? Look for the answer in 1 Peter 3:14 and Romans 8:28.

2. Genesis 50:20 says that what Satan means for harm, God can intend for good. When have you experienced this yourself or seen it in others' lives?

3. Fill in the blanks in the last sentence of the second paragraph of the section "How to Be Happy": "God _____ right _____."

4. What does the world say we need to do to be happy? And what does Scripture say? See Acts 20:35 and John 13:1–15.

5. What is one way to get your mind off of yourself when you are experiencing trials?

6. What does having a good attitude do to the devil?

7. How can being jealous of others give you a bad attitude? What are the three things you can do to combat this?

8. What does this statement mean: "Our attitude is the prophet of our future"?

How to Maintain a Good Attitude

1. What is the first way to maintain the right attitude when you find yourself in a mess?

2. Instead of praying for a life without trouble, how should you pray?

3. What is the second way to maintain the right attitude when you find yourself in a mess?

4. What situations has God brought you through in the past, and how does that encourage you to trust Him to bring you

through the troubles you face currently and the ones you may face in the future?

5. What is the third way to maintain the right attitude when you find yourself in a mess?

6. Have you ever failed to let your emotions subside before you decide? What did that experience teach you about making decisions?

7. What is the fourth way to maintain the right attitude when you find yourself in a mess?

8. Why are James 4:8 and Proverbs 3:5–6 encouraging to you?

9. What is the fifth way to maintain the right attitude when you find yourself in a mess?

10. Even if you are dealing with a negative situation right now, what are some things that are good and right in your life?

11. What are two scriptures that will help you draw close to God when you need comfort?

12. What is the best way to keep your situation in perspective?

13. Great things can happen during seasons of major hardship. Name some people who fit this description from the *Blessed in the Mess* book, the Bible, and your own life.

14. Based on what you learned in *Blessed in the Mess*, why do you think this statement is true: "If a person is truly great, their true greatness always emerges during crisis"?

15. What did you learn about maintaining a positive attitude from Katie Piper's story? What inspired you the most?

16. Fill in the blanks in the last sentence of chapter 8: "Nothing does more _____ to the devil's plans for our destruction and misery than _____ a _____ _____ amid a _____ _____."

CHAPTER 9

Stay Positive

1. What is one reason the Israelites may have made their journey through the wilderness harder than it needed to be?

2. Why can negative thinking limit what God can do in your life?

3. Do you know any naysayers like the ten Israelite spies who gave a negative report? What effect do they have on your faith and attitude?

4. Do you believe the way you see yourself affects how others see you? Do you have any examples of times when your attitude about yourself affected the way other people viewed you?

5. True or false: Being positive means you pretend your problems don't exist. Explain your answer.

6. According to Psalm 27:13–14 (AMPC), what should be our attitude while we are waiting on the Lord?

7. When our thoughts, emotions, and attitudes begin to sink as a result of problems we face, how can we interrupt their downward direction?

8. List the negative attitudes the Israelites displayed in their speech in Numbers 14:2–4. Ask God to protect you from speaking this way and engaging in negativity.

You Can Have All You See

1. What did God do for Abram when Abram allowed Lot to choose the best land? What can this story teach you about seeing with the eyes of faith?

2. Did you do the exercise in the section "You Can Have All You See," where you visualize a future without your problems? If not, do it now, and describe what your life could look like. How does this increase your faith?

3. Fill in the blanks in Ephesians 3:20 (AMPC): God "is able to... do superabundantly, far _____ and _____ all that we [dare] _____ or _____ [infinitely _____ our highest _____, _____, _____, _____, or _____].'"

4. Who or what is the main source of negativity in your life?

5. How does faith in God help you see beyond your problems?

6. Why is it best not to listen to the people who discourage you when God calls you to do something?

The Power of a Positive Mind

1. Fill in the blanks in the first sentence of the second paragraph of the section "The Power of a Positive Mind": "I've learned that _____ minds produce _____ lives, but _____ minds produce _____ lives." How have you found this to be true?

2. What did you learn from the story of the Roman soldier in Matthew 8:5–10? Why was Jesus so pleased with him?

3. When you ask God for something, do you fully expect Him to do what you requested? Search your heart, and if your

answer is no, ask His forgiveness and pray He will increase your faith.

4. What will steal our faith if we aren't careful to keep our thoughts filled with faith and confidence in God?

5. Some people have a negative attitude because they think it will help them avoid disappointment. But how could this attitude actually contribute to disappointment?

6. What kinds of things does Philippians 4:8 say you should be thinking about?

7. In what area or situation in your life do you struggle most to replace negative thoughts with positive ones? Ask God to help you and free you from this stronghold.

No Regrets

1. How do we feel if we have regrets?

2. What happens if we wallow in regret for too long?

3. Have you ever felt that, as a Christian, you're "supposed" to suffer and feel bad about yourself? What does John 10:10 say God wants for you?

4. I had to learn that work was not the only thing that gave me value. Have you ever felt that your value is based on what you do or produce?

5. Are you still living with guilt and regret for things you did years ago? Fill in the blanks in the second sentence of the third paragraph of the section "No Regrets": "But I have also learned how to _____, _____ for _____, _____ it, and _____ _____." How can you put these steps into practice in your life?

6. Every fruit of guilt is negative. What are three ways guilt affects us?

7. You may feel guilty, but God's Word says that once you have repented, God forgives your sin and removes the guilt (Hebrews 9:14). Based on 1 Peter 2:24–25, why does guilt serve no useful purpose in the Christian's life once they've repented?

8. Fill in the blanks in this sentence from the fourth paragraph of the section "No Regrets": "We may _____ grief about our sins, but we are not supposed to _____ _____ that grief."

9. What is the difference between godly sorrow and worldly sorrow?

10. How will letting go of regrets help you live with greater positivity?

CHAPTER 10

Remain Patient

1. In the opening quote for chapter 10, how does A. W. Tozer indicate that "problems patiently endured" help us? What does he say is the only way for problems to harm us?

2. How does patience, a fruit of the Spirit, grow?

3. Fill in the blanks in the first sentence of chapter 10: "Patience is not simply the _____ to _____; it includes our _____ and behavior _____ we wait."

4. On a scale of 1–10, with 1 being "I have no patience at all" and 10 being "I am the most patient person I know," how patient are you?

5. If you consider yourself an extremely patient person, what did you have to go through to reach that stage?

6. If you're still working to develop patience, what challenges are you facing as you try to keep a positive attitude while you wait?

7. According to James 1:2–3 (AMPC), why should we be joyful in all kinds of trials?

8. Why is patience also referred to as "long-suffering"?

9. Complete this sentence from the fifth paragraph of chapter 10: "Patience is a decision to _____ _____."

10. Have you reached the point of being constant—the same in difficult times as in good times? What work do you have left to do in this area?

What Happens When We Are Not Patient?

1. According to Luke 21:19, what is the attribute you need to possess your own soul and allow the Holy Spirit to lead you?
2. What three components does the soul consist of?
3. What happens if you don't possess your soul?
4. Based on the last sentence of the second paragraph of the section "What Happens When We Are Not Patient?," when does frustration occur?
5. Are you frustrated about anything right now? What is it?
6. How do you behave when you become frustrated instead of remaining patient? How does it affect your decisions? How does it impact the people in your life? How do others affect you when they act impatient with you?
7. What is your typical reaction when you can't get what you want? Do you wait on God, or do you take the matter into your own hands?
8. Think of a time when you tried to make something happen in your own effort, or works of the flesh. Did you notice a delay in God's plan coming to pass in that area? How did the experience teach you to practice patience the next time in order to receive God's blessing? If you're still working on this, ask God to help you to wait on His timing with a right attitude.
9. Why is it better to be patient than proud? And what are the two things we should do before making a plan?

10. Have you ever made a plan and asked God to bless it? How did that work out?

11. Which two qualities do you forfeit when you aren't patient, according to the first sentence of the sixth paragraph of the section "What Happens When We Are Not Patient?"

12. Impatience causes stress, and stress causes sickness. What symptoms have you or someone you know experienced related to this?

13. In this section there are several questions that can help you determine how you handle stress. Which situations cause you to lose your patience most quickly? How can you stay calm when you encounter them?

Enjoy the Moment

1. Are you the type of person who is always in a hurry, waiting for something to happen in the future so you can "be happy"? What are you missing when you live this way?

2. Why is being upset about what we don't have instead of enjoying what we do have one of life's tragedies?

3. How have you found this statement to be true: "The greatest present we can ever have is the present"?

4. Patience doesn't just happen. To become more patient, you have to practice. How can you practice patience today?

5. Fill in the blanks in these sentences from the fifth paragraph of the section "Enjoy the Moment": "And during our ordinary days, _____ things happen sometimes. When they do, we can exercise patience in the messes by letting the world do whatever it will while we remain _____ and _____."

6. Are there any moments—or people—in your life that you wish you'd enjoyed more instead of rushing through them? Describe them.

7. Is there anything going on in the present that you could be enjoying more instead of rushing through it? Are there people you could spend more quality time with? How will you do this?

8. How can people have joy in the tasks they have to do even when those tasks are not fun?

Never Give Up

1. Do you find yourself giving up easily—on your hopes and dreams, on others, or on yourself? Have other people given up on you? How could more patience have changed these outcomes? Commit to work on never giving up—with God's help.

2. Do you know someone who needs to change? Are you praying for God to do what needs to be done in that person?

3. What did you learn from the story "The Spider and the King"? Can you identify with any of it? Can you think of times when you could have kept going but gave up too soon?

4. What are the two things that can help you when you get depressed and feel like giving up?

5. Can you think of a circumstance you want to change? How might you need to change your attitude before the circumstance can change? What do you need to change in the "wineskin" of your attitude to be prepared for a new life (Mark 2:22)?

6. Have you ever lost something you wanted and thought all hope was gone but later on something even better happened? What

were the circumstances, and how did the situation increase your trust in God?

7. What did you learn about the dangers of impatience from the story of King Saul?

8. Do you live with a lot of regret and what-ifs? If so, ask God to help you stop looking at your past and start looking at your future. Commit to trust Him today for a better tomorrow.

Help in Building Patience

1. Read and meditate on the five scriptures in the section "Help in Building Patience." Which one could you memorize and meditate on often? Once your mind is renewed by this verse, commit to memorize another and then another until you've memorized all five.

Be Thankful

1. Fill in the blanks in this sentence from the first paragraph of chapter 11: "The more _____ we are, the more _____ our _____ are and the less access our _____ _____, Satan, has to our lives."

2. Do you often tell people that you're thankful for them? Who is one person you can thank in the next week for the blessing they've been in your life?

3. What is one positive way trials and trouble affect us?

4. If you're going through a painful or difficult time right now, are there things you can think of to be thankful for even in the midst of it? Thank God for them now.

Be Thankful on Purpose

1. Complete this first sentence of the section "Be Thankful on Purpose": "Complaining happens automatically if we don't _____."

2. What can you learn about anxiety and about prayer from Philippians 4:6?

3. Take a moment to think about all the blessings you take for granted, such as air to breathe, transportation, and running

water. How many other simple, common or ordinary things can you think of to thank God for?

4. Do you find yourself complaining, repenting, and recommitting to thankfulness over and over again? Don't stop repenting and recommitting to thankfulness. Keep doing it every time you realize you are not thankful for something. This will help you establish a habit of thankfulness.

What Is God's Will for My Life?

1. What does 1 Thessalonians 5:18–19 teach about God's will for your life? Was this the answer you were expecting, or were you looking for something more specific?

2. How could increasing your gratitude produce more specific guidance from the Holy Spirit in your life?

3. Have you ever observed someone going through extremely difficult or painful circumstances, yet remaining positive? How did this affect you?

4. In what situations do you find it challenging to practice thankfulness? How does Romans 8:28 encourage you?

5. Fill in the blanks in Psalm 34:1: "I _____ extol the Lord _____ _____ _____; his praise will _____ be on my lips."

Thank God Repeatedly for the Same Things

1. What blessings do you thank God for today, even if you have already thanked Him for them many, many times?

2. Do you have a request to make of God today? What can you thank Him for before you ask Him for anything?

3. Fill in the blanks in this sentence from the fourth paragraph of the section "Thank God Repeatedly for the Same Things": "Anytime you start to feel _____ or _____, start _____ _____ for the blessings in your life."

4. Why can getting something outside of God's will and timing be a problem? What can you learn about this from the Israelites' lusting for meat?

Thankful People Are Happy People

1. Fill in the blank in this sentence from the first paragraph of the section "Thankful People Are Happy People": "Everyone wants to feel _____."

2. What is one thing you can do regularly to make expressing gratitude to others a daily habit? Is there a call you could make, a card or email you could send, a gift you could give, a meal you could make, or some other way you could let someone know you appreciate them?

3. What do thankful people focus on?

4. Do you always need the next "thing" to continue being "happy"? How can practicing thankfulness for what you have now break that cycle?

Symptoms of a Lack of Gratitude

1. Here is the list of symptoms of a lack of gratitude. Put a checkmark by any that surprise you and take time to think about why they indicate a lack of thankfulness. Put a circle around any you are guilty of and ask God's forgiveness.

- negativity
- complaining
- selfishness
- an attitude of entitlement
- comparison
- jealousy
- pride
- self-pity

2. According to Jeremiah 17:9, why is it a good idea to regularly ask God to reveal any areas of your life that need work in this area?

3. When we hear ourselves complaining, it's a sign that we need to grow in what?

4. How can you better recognize complaining and stop it from creeping into your everyday discussions?

CHAPTER 12

Believe That God Is Bigger Than Your Problems

1. Why is it important to believe the statement "The way we think and what we believe can help us or defeat us"?
2. Complete Romans 5:20: "Where sin increased, _____
    _____."
3. According to 1 John 4:4, why is God greater than any problem you face? When have you come to the end of your abilities and needed Him to intervene? What happened?
4. Have you ever felt that your sins have disqualified you from being used by God? How can you renew your mind in this area and begin to believe again that He will use you?
5. What can you learn about God's greatness and power from Psalm 147:3–5 (ESV) and 1 Timothy 6:15–16 (ESV)?
6. Do you believe all things are possible with God (Matthew 19:26; Jeremiah 32:27)? When has He proven this to you?

God Loves Us and He Is Good

1. How do these verses encourage you in your relationship with God?
    - John 3:16
    - Romans 5:8
    - Romans 8:37–39

2. Fill in the blanks in this sentence from the last paragraph of the section "God Loves Us and He Is Good": "No _____ is big enough to _____ us from God's _____."

God's Love Defeats Your Enemies

1. If we truly believe God loves us, what else can we believe?

2. Have you ever said, "I know You love me, Lord"? Try doing this the next time you encounter a problem and are waiting for God to deliver you. How can this increase your faith?

3. What happens to Satan's plan of destruction each time we declare God's Word?

4. Why is God's love the answer to problems of the heart as well as the problems of the body?

5. If you are a fearful person, how does 1 John 4:18 give you hope?

6. Fill in the blanks in this sentence in the second-to-last paragraph of the section "God's Love Defeats Your Enemies": "Until we allow the _____ of God to _____ our souls, we can't receive _____ from anyone else, because we don't believe we are _____."

7. How has God proven to you that He is greater than anything that comes against you? In what situation do you need to remember His greatness today?

8. Do you know anyone who doubts God's love? How can you show them love, as Dave showed me?

God Is Good at All Times

1. In your own words, explain what Jonathan Edwards's quotation means: "There would be no manifestation of God's grace or true

goodness, if there was no sin to be pardoned, no misery to be saved from."

2. What situations in your life cause you to believe that God is good?

3. Why is Matthew 7:11 encouraging to you?

Watch Your Enemies Flee

1. What "enemies" (troubles) are you facing right now?

2. How do these verses encourage you as you face the enemies in your life?
    - Deuteronomy 28:7
    - Exodus 23:22
    - Luke 10:19 (NKJV)

3. Fill in the blanks in this sentence from the last paragraph of the section "Watch Your Enemies Flee": "Because _____ lives in you, there is no _____ you cannot _____ if you are walking in _____ to Him."

God Turns Messes into Miracles

1. Have you noticed a miraculous transformation in yourself since you believed in Jesus? Or have others noticed this in you? How have you changed?

2. Did your behavior change immediately when you were born again, or was it a process? What steps did you have to go through to see true change in yourself? Have you noticed this process in others?

3. What does Romans 12:2 mean when it says to "be transformed by the renewing of your mind"? What part does God's Word play in this process?

4. Why is 2 Corinthians 3:18 encouraging to you as God turns your mess into a miracle?

5. Based on the fourth paragraph of the section "God Turns Messes into Miracles," what three things do we need to do in addition to simply reading God's Word if we want our messes transformed into miracles?

From a Mess to a Miracle

1. How does the story of Saul's transformation encourage you in your faith?

2. What did you learn from the story of my father's transformation? How does this give you hope for yourself or any loved ones who need to change?

3. Why are life's tests necessary for us to have a testimony?

4. Do you have a testimony? Or are you still stuck in the "moanies"? How can you turn away from self-pity and use your troubles to bless others?

5. Count God's promises to you in Isaiah 41:10:
   1. "I am _____ _____."
   2. "I am _____ _____."
   3. "I will _____ you."
   4. "And _____ you."
   5. "I will _____ you with my _____ _____ _____."

6. How does Isaiah 41:10–13 encourage you?

7. What can God do with the things Satan intends to harm you?

No Weapon Formed against Me Shall Succeed

1. When something or someone comes against you, how does Isaiah 54:17 strengthen you?

2. Has God ever vindicated you regarding your enemies? What form did this take?

3. According to Matthew 5:44, what should you do when you need God to vindicate you?

4. Has anyone close to you ever hurt or betrayed you? Both Paul and Jesus knew this experience. What did they do, and how can you follow their example?

5. Fill in the blanks in the second-to-last sentence of the section "No Weapon Formed against Me Shall Succeed": "If you and I will _____ for the people who _____ us, God will take our _____ and turn it into our _____."

CHAPTER 13

Trust God When You Don't Understand

1. Can you identify with my friend's story about being angry with God? Why or why not?

2. Have you ever been falsely accused of something? How did you deal with it? Did it shake your faith or make it stronger?

3. Have you ever thought you knew better than God did in a situation? Take time to ask for and receive His forgiveness.

4. Fill in the blanks in the first sentence of the last paragraph of my friend's story: "I know that God can take our _____, _____, and _____, and gently _____ us through them." Do you believe this?

When We Don't Understand

1. Have you ever gone through a situation you didn't understand at the time but now understand and realize was valuable? What happened, and why are you now thankful for it?

2. Have you ever sacrificed something for God, fully expecting to be blessed, only to find yourself suffering lean times? How did God strengthen your trust in Him and prove Himself faithful in that situation?

3. According to 1 Corinthians 13:9, "we know in part." What unanswered questions do you have right now? How are you trusting God in the midst of them?
4. Have you ever tried to give God advice about what would be best for you? After you saw His real plan unfold, how did it compare with what you originally had in mind?
5. Isaiah 55:8–9 says God's thoughts are higher than ours. When have you experienced this?
6. Explain in your own words what this statement means to you: "If we don't like a good mystery, we are not going to enjoy our relationship with God."

Trust Brings Peace

1. What aspects of faith are mysteries to you?
2. We often try to figure things out because we want to be in control. On a scale of 1–10, with 1 being "Not very important at all" and 10 being "I want to understand and control everything in my life—and in other people's lives too," how important is being in control to you?
3. Do you spend a lot of time trying to figure out why bad things have happened to you? Why do you want to understand the bad more than the good?
4. Are you addicted to reasoning? Or are you able to have peace even when you don't understand everything happening to and around you?
5. How does Jesus' example of asking God a question that got no answer in Matthew 27:46 encourage you to trust God more in the darkness?

6. Have you found this statement to be true: "Sometimes, the more we know, the more unhappy we are"? How does this encourage you to trust what God chooses to help you understand—or not?

Suffering Leaves Many Questions

1. When did suffering first enter the world, and what brought it about?
2. Why is Revelation 21:4 an encouraging scripture to remember when going through suffering?
3. Why is suffering sometimes the only thing that will bring a person to God? Have you experienced this?
4. When you see bad things happening to good people, what is important for you to remember about God?

Our Chaotic World

1. What is the most important thing you can do to experience peace in the midst of our chaotic world?
2. Fill in the blanks in the last two sentences of the section "Our Chaotic World": "The _____ God gives is a peace that the _____ cannot _____ because it is not based on having to have all the _____. It is based on _____ _____, who does have all the answers."

What to Do Spiritually When You Don't Have Practical Answers for Your Problems

1. What are five spiritual things the Bible says you can do when you don't know how to solve your problems? Which can you start doing today?

2. What are the five practical things you can do when you don't know how to solve your problems? Which will be the easiest? The most challenging?

3. Remaining joyful during life's trials confuses the enemy and can hasten your victory. How can you enjoy your life in the midst of your problems?

4. Complete what Jesus says in John 16:33: "In this world you will have trouble. _____

_____."

Be Confident That You Always Triumph in Christ

1. What does it mean to you to know that, as a believer, you are destined to triumph over opposition?

2. How has God helped you triumph over some type of opposition?

3. Fill in the blanks in this sentence from paragraph 2 of chapter 14: "We _____ when the devil does his _____ and we come out of our trouble still loving _____ and loving _____, with our _____ even _____ than it was before the opposition came against us."

4. How can you train yourself to focus on the hope of victory instead of on your problems?

5. Why is hope important when you're facing opposition?

6. Hebrews 12:2 gives us important advice about facing opposition. What is it?

7. Think of some trials you have gone through. Did you maintain your love of God and people through them? If not, what tripped you up? What can you do in the future to keep a loving attitude?

8. Fill in the blanks in 2 Corinthians 2:14 (AMPC): "But thanks be to _____, Who in Christ _____ leads us in _____ [as trophies of Christ's victory] and through _____ spreads and makes evident the fragrance of the knowledge of God _____."

9. How do the trials I overcame in my life encourage you that you can do the same with God's help? Perhaps, you've suffered from one or more yourself. How did God show Himself faithful to you?

10. How can Romans 8:37 encourage you in a situation you are facing right now?

11. What is the danger of developing a victim mentality when going through difficult times? How does thinking about all Jesus suffered for you put your own problems in perspective?

In and through Christ

1. When we have victory, where does it come from?

2. How does Psalm 46:1–3 encourage you to see God as your "ever-present help in trouble"?

3. When you think of the difficulties the apostle Paul faced, how does it make you feel about your problems?

4. Why is 2 Corinthians 4:17–18 encouraging to you?

5. What is one reason God allows us to experience trials?

6. How is God teaching you not to trust in yourself but to trust in Him right now?

7. Why should prayer be your first course of action, not your last resort, when you face difficulties?

8. What do you find admirable about my friend's attitude after his wife died of cancer?

We Are More Than Conquerors

1. According to Romans 8:35–39, why shouldn't we let anyone or anything separate us from God's love?

2. In your own words, what does it mean to be more than a conqueror?

3. Why is it important to have a victorious mindset? If you still fret over problems like I once did, how can meditating on Romans 8:31 and Deuteronomy 20:4 help you?

God's Timing and His Ways

1. Of the five positive statements you can say to encourage yourself while waiting for your victory, which one or ones do you need to focus on most right now? How can you remind yourself to make these declarations?

2. When the enemy fills your mind with negativity, and you begin to verbalize it, how can you defeat him?

3. Why is making negative statements about yourself counterproductive?

Trust God for Favor

1. What is God's favor?

2. How have you experienced God's favor in your life?

3. According to the end of the second paragraph of the section "Trust God for Favor," what are three ways you can release your faith for God's favor in your life?

4. How do the Bible accounts of people receiving favor from God encourage you?

5. Is it possible to deserve God's favor?

6. In what situation will you ask God to give you His favor today?

Just Ask

1. The opening quote for chapter 15, by Teresa of Avila, says, "You pay God a great compliment by asking great things of Him." What "great thing" could you ask God for today?

2. What's the worst thing that can happen if you ask God for something that isn't in His will for you?

3. Reflect on this statement: "God has already provided *every* spiritual blessing in Christ, and He is simply waiting for us to ask to receive them." What are some spiritual blessings you could ask Him for today?

4. Fill in the blanks in this sentence from the second-to-last paragraph of the opening section of chapter 15: "Always _____ that He wants to bless you not because _____ are good but because _____ is good."

5. Psalm 37:4 puts a condition on receiving the desires of our hearts. What is it?

God Is a Giving God

1. In the context of giving, what does John 3:16 mean to you?

2. Do you believe that God, like a good parent, always does what's best for you? When have you experienced this?

3. Fill in the blanks in this sentence from the second paragraph of the section "God Is a Giving God": "Ask Him for _____, and be _____ with what He gives you, knowing that He always does what is _____ for you."

4. According to Philippians 4:19, why is it okay to ask God for money if you need it?

5. Is it possible to ask God for something too big? Why not?

I Don't Deserve That!

1. Are you afraid to ask God for big things because you don't feel you deserve them? How does Hebrews 4:15–16 describe the attitude we should have when approaching God's throne?

2. How does this statement encourage you and set you free: "Because we know that God loves us, we can go boldly to His throne and ask for whatever we need, even when we know we are far from perfect in our behavior"?

3. Are you sometimes afraid to ask God for things because you know you're not yet where you should be in your walk with Him? Certainly the apostles must have felt the same way. Yet John 15:3 teaches that they were already "clean." What understanding helped me to trust that I can boldly approach God's throne and ask for His help?

4. Do you have a heart after God yet still have weaknesses you are working through? Will this keep you from receiving the blessings God wants to give you?

5. How does this statement set you free from trying to earn God's blessings: "We don't get what we deserve, but we share in what Jesus deserves"?

6. What does it mean for you to be a "co-heir" with Jesus (Romans 8:17)? How is your inheritance from God similar to an earthly will?

7. What encouragement do you find in Ephesians 3:12 (AMPC) and 1 John 5:14 (AMPC)?

8. Think of one big thing you want right now and have the courage to ask God for it, fully expecting an answer.

Ask God to Turn Your Trouble into a Blessing

1. Go ahead and do as the first sentence of the section "Ask God to Turn Your Trouble into a Blessing" instructs: "Take a step of faith and ask God to take your trouble (mess) and make it a blessing."

2. If you caused part of the mess you are currently in, why is Romans 8:28 encouraging to you?

3. What are the two parts to God's promises?

4. Fill in the blanks in the last phrase of the third paragraph in the section "Ask God to Turn Your Trouble into a Blessing": "If we expect radical and outrageous _____, we should give God radical and outrageous _____."

5. What three simple things can you do to grow in obedience to God?

6. Why is keeping your heart grateful and free from offense so important in receiving God's blessing?

7. Share what these statements mean to you: "We don't have to chase things. Instead, we can chase God, and the things that are right for us will be given at the proper time."

CHAPTER 16

How to Be Blessed and Have Less of a Mess

1. What did Solomon conclude is the source of happiness in Ecclesiastes 12:13 (AMPC)? Have you come to this conclusion yourself yet, or are you still trying to make yourself happy with other things?
2. What does it mean to be "blessed" according to Matthew 5:3 (AMPC)? Does this describe your life? Why or why not?
3. What does it mean to prosper?

What Do We Really Want?

1. Why is spiritual prosperity more important than money and possessions?
2. Have you ever thought material things would bring you happiness and realized you really needed spiritual satisfaction? How did you figure that out?
3. What are some of the spiritual blessings that are important to you? Why is obedience to God the key to receiving them?
4. What one theme repeats itself in the Old Testament, explaining why the Israelites were blessed or not blessed?
5. How has obedience to God been a key to blessings in your life?
6. What is the difference between trying to earn God's blessings and being rewarded for our obedience to Him?

7. According to Hebrews 11:6, what is necessary to please God?
8. Are you earnestly seeking God, as taught in Hebrews 11:6? If not, how can you grow in seeking Him earnestly?

Radical Obedience and Outrageous Blessings

1. Has God ever asked you to do something that seemed radical? What was it, and what outrageous blessing came to you afterward?
2. According to 1 Corinthians 2:9, what has God stored up for those who love and obey Him?
3. What are some examples of when God has done "exceedingly abundantly above" what you've asked of Him (Ephesians 3:20)?
4. What promise does Luke 6:38 (AMPC) make to those who give?
5. What are some things the Bible teaches us to continue doing based on the following scriptures?
    - John 8:31 KJV
    - John 15:9 KJV
    - Acts 13:43 NKJV
    - Acts 14:22 NKJV
    - Colossians 4:2 NKJV
    - 2 Timothy 3:14 NKJV
    - Hebrews 13:1 NKJV

Radical Obedience

1. Have you ever known anyone who followed God in ways that seemed radical or beyond the scope of day-to-day obedience? What happened?

2. Fill in the blanks in the last sentence of the section "Radical Obedience": "Part of the reason God asks us to take steps of _____ _____ is that He is _____ our level of_____ ___ _____, and_____ us to _____ Him."

Biblical Men and Women Who Radically Obeyed God

1. What can you learn from Noah's example of building the ark? How would you have responded in that situation?
2. What inspires you about Daniel and his loyalty to God?
3. Have you, like Abram, had to leave a place you knew and go to a new location in order to obey God? What blessings did you find in the new place?
4. Which radically obedient people in the Bible do you admire the most, and why?
5. Jesus is the most radically obedient person in the entire Bible. What did He do that fits this description, and what was His outrageous blessing? How does this inspire your faith?
6. How does Romans 2:11 encourage you to believe that God can bless you, just as He blessed the radically obedient people we read about in the Bible?
7. How do you think radical obedience can lead to less of a mess in your life?
8. How do you believe God is asking you to grow in obedience in this season of your life? With His help, don't delay; start today.

PART 3

The Beatitudes: Keys to Blessing

CHAPTER 17

The First and Second Beatitudes

1. What does the English word *beatitude* mean, according to the Cambridge Dictionary?
2. The third-to-last paragraph of the first section of chapter 17 includes a summary of what I have learned about the Beatitudes. Complete this sentence: "I would say that the Beatitudes are _____

   _____

   _____

   _____."

1. Blessed Are the Poor in Spirit

1. Fill in the blanks of the first beatitude:

Blessed (_____, to be envied, and spiritually prosperous—with _____ and satisfaction in God's favor and salvation, regardless of their _____ conditions) are the _____ in _____ (the _____, who rate themselves insignificant), for theirs is the _____ of _____!

Matthew 5:3 AMPC

2. The poor in spirit are humble. What do the following scriptures teach about humility?
    - Ephesians 4:2 (NIV)
    - Colossians 3:12 (NIV)
    - 1 Peter 5:5 (NKJV)

3. What is the opposite of humility? And why can this be considered the root of all evil and beginning of sin?

4. Fill in the blanks in these sentences from the second paragraph under the heading "Pride: The Opposite of Humility": "Pride causes us to _____ ourselves with other people, but those who are _____ _____ _____ avoid this because they see no _____ for _____. The _____ do not _____ themselves with anyone else because they are _____ to be who God made them to be and to exercise the _____ He has given them."

5. According to 1 Peter 5:6, if we humble ourselves, what will God do?

6. Do you think you know any truly humble people? What signs of humility do you see in them?

7. Proverbs 16:18 teaches that pride comes before what?

8. Why is it important to treat all people well and respectfully?

9. What does Matthew 11:29 teach about Jesus?

2. Blessed Are Those Who Mourn

1. Fill in the blanks in the second beatitude:

Blessed and enviably happy [with a _____ produced by the experience of God's favor and especially conditioned by

the revelation of His matchless _____] are those who
_____, for they shall be _____!

Matthew 5:4 AMPC

2. Fill in the blanks in the first paragraph of the section "Blessed Are Those Who Mourn": "If we believe that God's _____ and _____ are greater than any _____ or _____, we can experience _____ in the midst of _____."

3. What losses or situations in your life have caused you to mourn?

4. Have you known anyone who has suffered a great loss but has received God's comfort? What did you observe in that person's attitude or about their faith?

5. Have you known anyone, like Jacob, who refused to be comforted, even over time? How did that play out?

6. What does 2 Corinthians 1:3–4 teach about God?

7. Have you ever experienced God's comfort when going through a loss of your own? In what ways did that enable you to comfort others?

8. What are some of the things that happen to good people when bad things happen to them? Have you experienced any of these?

9. Are there things you have lost or suffered that you mourned at the time and later realized that although God didn't cause them, He used them to draw you closer to Himself? What were they?

10. Would you rather have God's comfort or your self-pity? What do you need to sacrifice to have His comfort?

11. Fill in the blanks in the second to the last sentence in the third paragraph under the heading "The Folly of Self-Pity": "We can be _____ or _____, but we cannot be both."

12. What is self-pity rooted in?

13. When you look at the signs of self-pity, do you see any that you exhibit? If so, confess them to God and ask for His forgiveness and help in overcoming them.

14. What did you learn from my example of trusting God in the midst of my back problem? How can you take similar steps as you deal with your problems?

15. According to the second sentence under the heading "Find Comfort in Hope," what is hope?

16. What good thing are you expecting God to do in your life?

17. Why do these scriptures encourage you to have hope?
    - Romans 8:28
    - Philippians 4:13
    - 1 Corinthians 10:13
    - Psalm 91:15
    - Psalm 34:19

18. What does John 16:7 teach about the Holy Spirit?

The Third and Fourth Beatitudes

3. Blessed Are the Meek

1. Fill in the blanks in the third beatitude:

Blessed (_____, blithesome, joyous, spiritually prosperous—with life-joy and _____ in God's favor and salvation, regardless of their outward conditions) are the _____ (the mild, patient, _____), for they shall _____ _____ _____!

Matthew 5:5 AMPC

2. According to the first sentence of chapter 18, what three words describe what it means to be meek?
3. Fill in the blanks in this sentence from the first paragraph in the section "Blessed Are the Meek": "Meekness is often misunderstood as _____, but it is actually _____ under _____."
4. How did Jesus demonstrate meekness in the garden of Gethsemane?
5. According to the third paragraph of the section "Blessed Are the Meek," meekness is an attitude that says what?

6. What can you learn from Jesus's example of meekness in 1 Peter 2:23?

7. If you are waiting for God to bring justice into your life, how do Romans 12:19 and Hebrews 10:30 encourage you?

8. Why is this statement true: "If we will wait on God when we are mistreated, the vindication He gives will be much sweeter than any we could ever obtain for ourselves"?

9. Have you ever exercised the power of restraint in a situation and seen God do something amazing to vindicate you? What happened?

10. Sometimes we need to speak up and refuse to allow people to take advantage of us. Whose good should we have in mind when we do this?

11. If you, like me, grew up fighting injustice in your own family, you may consider restraining yourself when wronged as a sign of weakness and "letting them get away with it." How could Jesus' example of meekness inspire you to wait on God's timing vs. taking matters into your own hands?

12. How did Jesus conduct Himself when He was accused of doing wrong?

13. How have you observed this statement to be true: "The meeker people are, the more powerful they are"? How does Jesus provide an example of this?

14. What is the difference between being a laborer and being an inheritor? Which one are you?

15. In what ways have you tried to do what only God can do? What affect has that had on you and on the situations you've tried to change?

16. Fill in the blanks in this sentence from the second paragraph under the heading "Are You a Laborer or an Inheritor?": "God wants us to be _____ with what we _____

while we _____ on Him to give us more—in His _____ and in His _____."

17. Have you learned to be content, as Paul writes about in Philippians 4:11–12? What brought you to this place?

18. What is the only way we can learn to be content?

19. Even though God gives us His Word to teach us how to live, we don't always obey it. Have you ever had to find out the hard way that God's ways are best? What happened?

20. What are some of the blessings God gives us that we cannot earn or buy with our works (fleshly efforts)?

21. Why is receiving correction the pathway to growth and advancement?

22. When we want to move forward in life but feel stuck, the reason is usually one of two things. What are they?

23. Why does God show us our weaknesses?

24. In what ways can God's correction be viewed as positive?

25. If God can't get your attention Himself, He will use other means. In what ways has He used other people to prompt a change in your behavior?

26. How did God use the prophet Jonah's circumstances to get his attention? When have you experienced God using your circumstances to encourage your obedience?

4. Blessed Are Those Who Hunger and Thirst for Righteousness

1. Fill in the blanks of the fourth beatitude:

Blessed and fortunate and happy and _____ _____ (in that state in which the born-again child of

God enjoys His _____ and _____) are those who _____ and _____ for righteousness (uprightness and right standing with God), for they shall be _____ _____!

Matthew 5:6 AMPC

2. What does *righteousness* mean?
3. On a scale of 1–10, how hungry and thirsty for righteousness are you, with 1 being "I don't think about righteousness very much" and 10 being "I live with a keen recognition of my deep spiritual need for righteousness"?
4. Fill in the blanks in Psalm 42:1–2: "As the deer _____ for streams of water, so _____ _____ pants for you, my _____. My soul _____ for God, for the _____ God. When can I go and _____ with God?"
5. According to Philippians 3:9, on what basis can we have "the righteousness that comes from God"?
6. What are the two types of righteousness? Which one are you practicing?
7. Why did God give the law, according to Romans 3:20–25 and Galatians 3:19–27?
8. Under the Old Testament law, what did animal sacrifices accomplish?
9. What is the payment for sin under the New Covenant?
10. In your own words, what does 2 Corinthians 5:21 (AMPC) mean?
11. Have you ever asked God this question: "How can I know when I have done enough?" What prompted your need to know this?

12. Fill in the blanks in these sentences from the first paragraph under the heading "When Have I Done Enough?": "To _____ and _____ for righteousness refers to the _____ with which one _____ to live righteously. In other words, it is not merely a _____ _____ but an _____ _____ to please _____, one that is _____ enough to affect our _____."

13. God doesn't want your effort; He wants your faith. What does this mean? How can knowing this help you live in true righteousness?

14. According to 2 Corinthians 5:17, when does a person become new in Christ?

15. Complete the last sentence in paragraph 3 under the heading "When Have I Done Enough?": "Right standing with God is

_____

_____

_____."

16. What does this statement mean: "God never expects us to produce something unless He first gives it to us"? How does this relate to the following areas:
    • Righteousness
    • Holiness
    • Forgiveness
    • Mercy

17. According to the first sentence of the fifth paragraph under the heading "When Have I Done Enough?," what are the three things we must do before we can do all God wants us to do?

    1. _____ who we are in Christ.

    2. _____ what He has given us.

    3. _____ it by faith.

18. According to Hebrews 11:1, what is faith?

19. How do we receive God's promises as a reality in our lives?

20. Fill in the blanks in this sentence from the last paragraph of chapter 18: "You have _____ enough when you sincerely _____."

CHAPTER 19

The Fifth and Sixth Beatitudes

5. Blessed Are the Merciful

1. Fill in the blanks of the fifth beatitude:

Blessed (happy, to be envied, and spiritually prosperous—
with _____ and _____ in God's favor and
salvation, regardless of their _____ conditions) are the
_____, for they shall _____ _____!

Matthew 5:7 AMPC

2. Why do we all need mercy?
3. What is the best way for us to be given mercy?
4. Based on Lamentations 3:22–23 (NKJV), when can we expect
   God's mercies in our lives?
5. Why are you personally thankful for God's mercy?
6. Why is mercy better than sacrifice? What are some ways you
   can show more mercy to those around you instead of requiring
   something from them when they make mistakes, fail, offend,
   or hurt you?
7. If you had to write a definition of mercy based on what you read in
   the first several paragraphs of chapter 19, how would you define it?

8. Complete this sentence from the second-to-last paragraph before the header "We Reap What We Sow." Referring to Jesus, it says: "He didn't merely feel sorry for hurting people; _____

_____

_____."

9. Has God shown you mercy when you didn't deserve it? How did you react?

10. Has another human being ever been merciful to you when you knew you didn't deserve mercy? What happened, and how did their expression of mercy affect you?

11. Is there someone in your life to whom you can be merciful this week? Ask God to show you how to freely give mercy to them, as He has freely given mercy to you.

12. In what ways did Jesus show mercy? How does His compassion inspire you to show mercy and compassion?

13. The biblical concept of mercy goes beyond forgiveness and withholding punishment. What are some examples?

14. What does it mean to reap what you sow? Is there any way to avoid reaping what you sow?

15. How have you seen the principle of sowing and reaping work in your life or in someone else's life? How have you seen it work in both positive and negative ways?

16. Describe the harvest you want to reap in your life. To receive that, what do you need to sow *less* of, and what do you need to sow *more* of?

17. Fill in the blanks in the first part of Luke 6:37: "Do not _____, and you will not be _____. Do not _____, and you will not be _____."

18. Fill in the blanks in the second part of Luke 6:37 and in Luke 6:38: "Forgive, and you will be _____. Give, and it

will be _____ to _____. A good measure, pressed down, shaken together and running over, will be poured into your lap. For with the _____ you use, it will be _____ to you."

19. Why does selfishness lead to unhappiness? And why does caring for others bring joy? How does your experience prove this?

20. Fill in the blanks in this sentence from the fourth paragraph under the heading "The Blessing of Caring for Others": "Mercy does not look _____ at what a person has _____ but takes time to see _____ they did it."

21. Based on Lamentations 3:22–23, what would happen to us if God did not show us mercy?

22. Are you the type of person who criticizes others or likes to correct people or offer unsolicited advice about how they can improve? What does James 2:13 say about this type of attitude?

23. According to Colossians 3:12 (ESV), if it doesn't come naturally to you, you can still choose to "put on" mercy. What characteristics of mercy could you put into practice based on this verse?

24. What practical lessons can you learn from the story of the Good Samaritan (Luke 10:30–32)?

25. Do you ever feel too busy to help people who need help? How could you be more intentional about looking for opportunities to show mercy to people?

26. According to Proverbs 11:17 (NKJV), how does mercy affect a person who is merciful?

27. Can you think of someone who needs mercy right now? Who is it, and what can you do for them? Don't miss out on the blessing of showing mercy.

6. Blessed Are the Pure in Heart

1. Fill in the blanks of the sixth beatitude:

   Blessed (happy, enviably fortunate, and spiritually prosperous—possessing the _____ produced by the experience of God's _____ and especially conditioned by the revelation of His _____, regardless of their outward conditions) are the _____ _____ _____, for they shall _____ _____!

                                                           Matthew 5:8 AMPC

2. What does it mean to "see God"?
3. According to Matthew Henry's commentary on Matthew 5:8, where does true Christianity lie?
4. What are some characteristics of the "pure in heart"? Would you describe yourself this way? Why or why not?
5. Can you make yourself pure in heart? If not, who does this work?
6. How do you receive purity of heart?
7. Fill in the blanks in this sentence from the first paragraph under the heading "Pure-Hearted and Powerful": "Having a pure heart starts with _____ _____ to our _____, because from our _____ come our _____, our _____, our _____, and our _____.
8. Psalm 51:6 teaches us to have truth in our inner being. What does this mean to you? Is there a way you can grow in having truth in your inner being?

9. Purity of heart does not come naturally to most people. According to 1 Thessalonians 4:3, why should you work toward achieving it?

10. Complete this first sentence under the heading "Motives": "Our motives refer to _____ _____."

11. If we are motivated to do good works so other people will see us, what will happen, according to Matthew 6:1?

12. What should our motive be for the good things we do?

13. Matthew 6:1 and 1 Corinthians 3:12–15 warn about the danger of impure motives. Why do you need to examine your motives, even when you think you are doing good?

CHAPTER 20

The Seventh and Eighth Beatitudes

7. Blessed Are Those Who Make and Maintain Peace

1. Fill in the blanks of the seventh beatitude:

Blessed (enjoying _____ happiness, spiritually prosperous—with life-joy and satisfaction in God's favor and salvation, regardless of their outward conditions) are the _____ and _____ of _____, for they shall be _____ the sons of _____!

Matthew 5:9 AMPC

2. Fill in the blanks in this sentence from the first paragraph of the section "Blessed Are Those Who Make and Maintain Peace": "People who are spiritually _____ could be defined as those who no longer act based on how they _____, what they _____, or what they _____, but they are _____ to _____ _____ in every possible way."

3. How does the Bible characterize people who are immature?

4. Why does being a peacemaker require spiritual maturity?

5. How does a mature person's behavior differ from that of an infant in Christ, as expressed in 1 Corinthians 3:1–3?

6. On a scale of 1–10, with 1 being "I'm just starting to grow spiritually" and 10 being "I haven't fully arrived, but I have developed some characteristics of spiritual maturity," where are you? Wherever you are, there's always room for improvement with God's help.

7. In 1 Corinthians 3:1–3, why does Paul address his readers as "mere infants"?

8. Do you believe that peacemakers are powerful? Name some people who are powerful because they are peaceful.

9. What does James 1:20 teach about anger?

10. How do you react in a disagreement? Are you the first to be offended or the first to apologize? What can you do to grow in your ability to make and maintain peace?

11. The apostle Paul teaches in 2 Timothy 2:23 not to "have anything to do with foolish and stupid arguments" because "they produce quarrels." In what situations have you seen this happen? How can you avoid getting embroiled in such controversies and disagreements?

12. The early Christians mentioned in the Book of Acts had problems, as all people do. According to the last phrase of the first paragraph of the section "Know Peace, Know Power," how did they handle their problems?

13. Why is it important to keep strife out of your life?

14. What aspects of your life do you feel are most prone to strife? How can you make and maintain peace better in these areas?

15. What is the secret to having peace with other people?

16. According to the second paragraph under the heading "Peace with God," what two things happen if we don't walk in obedience to God's commands?

17. Do you start your day asking God to forgive any sins you committed in word, thought, or deed? If you want peace with God, I encourage you to start doing this. Then repent and thank God for His forgiveness.

18. How can we have peace with ourselves?

19. Complete this sentence from the first paragraph under the heading "Peace with Ourselves": "Not liking yourself is equivalent to _____

    _____

    _____."

20. Fill in the blanks in this sentence from the first paragraph under the heading "Peace with Ourselves": "You are _____ and _____ intended to be like someone else, so be diligent in _____ the _____ to _____ yourself with _____ _____."

21. What can you learn about yourself from the following Bible verses?
    • Romans 3:23
    • Romans 3:24

22. Why is it so important that you love and accept yourself so that you will be able to love others? If you struggle with this, what holds you back from loving and accepting yourself? Ask God to help you with this.

23. Fill in the blanks in this sentence from the second-to-last paragraph under the heading "Peace with Ourselves": "I focus on my _____ and pray about my _____."

8. Blessed Are Those Who Are Persecuted

1. Fill in the blanks of the eighth beatitude:

Blessed and _____ and enviably fortunate and spiritually prosperous (in the state in which the _____ child of God enjoys and finds satisfaction in God's favor and salvation, regardless of his outward conditions) are those who are _____ for _____ sake (for _____ and _____ right), for theirs is the _____ of _____! _____ (happy, to be envied, and spiritually prosperous—with life-joy and satisfaction in God's favor and salvation, _____ of your outward conditions) are you when people _____ you and _____ you and say all kinds of evil things against you _____ on My account. Be _____ and supremely _____, for your _____ in heaven is _____ (strong and intense), for in this same way people persecuted the prophets who were before you.

Matthew 5:10–12 AMPC

2. How can we consider ourselves blessed when we are being persecuted for doing what is right?

3. Have you ever been persecuted in some way because of your faith? What happened?

4. Have you ever witnessed a fellow believer being persecuted for their faith? How did you help?

5. Can you identify with the experience of losing friends or falling out with family members as a result of becoming a Christian or obeying God's leading in your life? What happened?

6. If you have suffered ridicule or lost relationships because of your faith, have you forgiven the people who hurt you? There's no better time than now to forgive them and ask God to bless them and draw them to Himself.

7. How might your faith cause you to make different choices than you have made in the past? Remember, if people don't accept you because of this, it may be the result of the Holy Spirit's conviction in their hearts.

8. If you haven't noticed any persecution in your life as a Christian, are there ways in which you have become lukewarm in your faith? What are they? How can you surrender more fully to God?

9. Should you be surprised when you face trials? Why or why not?

10. Fill in the blanks in this sentence from the first paragraph under the heading "We Are Blessed When We Suffer": "We never truly know how _____ our faith is until some _____ comes along to _____ it."

11. What is the reason 1 Peter 4:12 says fiery ordeals may come into your life?

12. When you feel ignored or persecuted in some way because of your faith, should you defend yourself?

13. Why is 2 Thessalonians 1:6–7 an encouraging Scripture passage?

14. In the second-to-last paragraph under the heading "We Are Blessed When We Suffer," I mention that I didn't like 1 Peter 2:19–20 when I first read it. Complete this sentence: "But now I understand that it isn't the suffering that pleases God; _____ _____ _____ _____."

15. Fill in the blanks from this sentence in the second-to-last paragraph under the heading "We Are Blessed When We Suffer": "Anyone can have a _____ _____ when everything is going their way, but _____

_____ is required to bear with _____ that is _____."

16. According to 1 Peter 2:21 (AMPC), when we suffer, whose personal example should we follow?

17. Do you believe you have participated "in the sufferings of Christ" (1 Peter 4:13)? Based on the list under the heading "Types of Persecution," what have you suffered?

18. Do you think of yourself as blessed and worthy of reward when you suffer for the sake of Christ? How does focusing on the fact that suffering brings a reward change your perspective on suffering?

19. According to Psalm 103:6, what does God do for those who are oppressed?

The Doorway to Blessings

1. Joseph Addison's quotation at the beginning of chapter 21 says, "A contented mind is the greatest blessing a man can enjoy in this world." What blessings have you experienced as a result of a contented mind?

2. What are some of the simple blessings you have that you may not think about often?

3. What is one doorway to more blessings in your life?

4. Fill in the blanks in this sentence from the second paragraph of chapter 21: "One thing is for sure, it is not our _____ —good or bad—that determine our level of _____; it is our _____ of those _____."

5. How have you observed this statement to be true: "Someone with a positive attitude can have negative circumstances and be happier than someone with a negative attitude and positive circumstances"?

6. What steals or blocks our blessings?

7. When have you been tempted to compromise and do a little less than what was right? What was the result?

8. What does God bless, based on these scriptures:
   - Joshua 1:8
   - Isaiah 1:19
   - Luke 5:1–10

9. What are five reasons people hated Jesus? Have you ever done right and expected a reward but none came? How does Galatians 6:9 encourage you?

10. In the story of Cain and Abel in Genesis 4:1–16, what characteristics did Cain display?

11. Have you ever known anyone who, like Cain, wanted the glory for something but did not want to make the sacrifice needed to accomplish the goal? What were the circumstances?

12. What did you learn from Moses's example of choosing suffering in Hebrews 11:24–25?

13. Do you think you would have done what Moses did if you were living in luxury in Pharaoh's palace? Why or why not?

Waiting for the Reward

1. Fill in the blanks in these sentences from the first paragraph of the section "Waiting for the Reward": "Don't do what is right to get a _____; do it because it is _____ and because you _____ _____. And let _____ take care of _____ in _____ _____ and according to _____ _____."

2. How does greed open the door to compromise? When have you witnessed or experienced this?

3. What is the best antidote for greed?

What Rewards Can We Expect?

1. As a reminder, what does Isaiah 61:7 say?

2. What does obedience to God always involve?

3. On a scale of 1–10, with 1 being "not at all" and 10 being "I can't think of any unforgiveness I hold toward anyone," how are you doing right now in the area of forgiving those who have hurt or offended you?

4. Doing things God's way brings various rewards. What are eight common rewards we can expect?

5. How can focusing on the rewards God gives help you overcome any reluctance to obey God completely?

6. What is the biggest reward of all?

7. What reward does Psalm 5:12 mention?

8. According to James 1:12, what reward does "the one who perseveres under trial because, having stood the test" receive?

9. What is the reward for diligence, according to Proverbs 12:24?

10. What kind of rewards do Deuteronomy 15:10 and Matthew 6:3–4 promise?

11. What kind of reward can we expect based on 1 John 3:21–22?

12. What does Psalm 119:165 promise to those who love God's law?

13. What is our final reward? What does Revelation 21:4 promise about this reward?

14. According to Romans 8:28, no matter what happens in your life, what can God do with it?

15. Do you believe that God can bless you in the midst of any mess you currently face and the ones you may go through in the future?

CONCLUSION

If you have read *Blessed in the Mess* and worked your way through this study guide, you have learned that life's messes are inevitable. Those messes may include job stress, family conflict, disappointment and other types of emotional pain, financial problems, a child struggling in school, a young person addicted to drugs or alcohol, and many other difficult situations. Jesus says that in the world we will have tribulation, but that we can be of good cheer because He has overcome the world (John 16:33). There is no way to avoid life's messes, but as we walk with God and obey His Word, we can find many ways to be blessed in the midst of them.

Many people make the mistake of trying to get *out* of their messes when they would benefit much more if they learned how to *go through* them. As you have learned through reading *Blessed in the Mess* and through your work in this study guide, dealing with life's difficulties has many benefits for us. When we face them with God's help, we become stronger people and more effective Christians. We grow closer to God, and we become more like Jesus.

I pray this study guide has equipped you to be more blessed in the midst of a mess than you ever thought you could be and to encourage and help people around you as they go through life's challenges.

Always remember, in Christ you are more than a conqueror, and nothing that happens on this earth can ever separate you from His love (Romans 8:37–39).

Do you have a real relationship with Jesus?

God loves you! He created you to be a special, unique, one-of-a-kind individual, and He has a specific purpose and plan for your life. And through a personal relationship with your Creator—God—you can discover a way of life that will truly satisfy your soul.

No matter who you are, what you've done, or where you are in your life right now, God's love and grace are greater than your sin—your mistakes. Jesus willingly gave His life so you can receive forgiveness from God and have new life in Him. He's just waiting for you to invite Him to be your Savior and Lord.

If you are ready to commit your life to Jesus and follow Him, all you have to do is ask Him to forgive your sins and give you a fresh start in the life you are meant to live. Begin by praying this prayer...

Lord Jesus, thank You for giving Your life for me and forgiving me of my sins so I can have a personal relationship with You. I am sincerely sorry for the mistakes I've made, and I know I need You to help me live right.

Your Word says in Romans 10:9, "If you declare with your mouth, 'Jesus is Lord,' and believe in your heart that God raised him from the dead, you will be saved" (NIV). I believe You are the Son of God and confess You as my Savior and Lord. Take me just as I am, and work in my heart, making me the person You want me to be. I want to live for You, Jesus, and I am so grateful that You are giving me a fresh start in my new life with You today.

I love You, Jesus!

It's so amazing to know that God loves us so much! He wants to have a deep, intimate relationship with us that grows every day as we spend time with Him in prayer and Bible study. And we want to encourage you in your new life in Christ.

Please visit joycemeyer.org/howtoknowJesus to request Joyce's book *A New Way of Living*, which is our gift to you. We also have other free resources online to help you make progress in pursuing everything God has for you.

Congratulations on your fresh start in your life in Christ! We hope to hear from you soon.

ABOUT THE AUTHOR

Joyce Meyer is one of the world's leading practical Bible teachers and a *New York Times* bestselling author. Joyce's books have helped millions of people find hope and restoration through Jesus Christ. Joyce's program, *Enjoying Everyday Life*, is broadcast on television, radio, and online to millions worldwide in over one hundred languages.

Through Joyce Meyer Ministries, Joyce teaches internationally on a number of topics with a particular focus on how the Word of God applies to our everyday lives. Her candid communication style allows her to share openly and practically about her experiences so others can apply what she has learned to their lives.

Joyce has authored more than 140 books, which have been translated into more than 160 languages, and over 39 million of her books have been distributed worldwide. Bestsellers include *Power Thoughts*; *The Confident Woman*; *Look Great, Feel Great*; *Starting Your Day Right*; *Ending Your Day Right*; *Approval Addiction*; *How to Hear from God*; *Beauty for Ashes*; and *Battlefield of the Mind*.

Joyce's passion to help people who are hurting is foundational to the vision of Hand of Hope, the missions arm of Joyce Meyer Ministries. Each year Hand of Hope provides millions of meals for the hungry and malnourished, installs freshwater wells in poor and remote areas, provides critical relief after natural disasters, and offers free medical and dental care to thousands through their hospitals and clinics worldwide. Through Project GRL, women and children are rescued from human trafficking and provided safe places to receive an education, nutritious meals, and the love of God.

JOYCE MEYER MINISTRIES
U.S. & FOREIGN OFFICE ADDRESSES

Joyce Meyer Ministries
P.O. Box 655
Fenton, MO 63026
USA
(636) 349-0303

Joyce Meyer Ministries—Canada
P.O. Box 7700
Vancouver, BC V6B 4E2
Canada
(800) 868-1002

Joyce Meyer Ministries—Australia
Locked Bag 77
Mansfield Delivery Centre·
Queensland 4122
Australia
(07) 3349 1200

Joyce Meyer Ministries—England
P.O. Box 1549
Windsor SL4 1GT
United Kingdom
01753 831102

Joyce Meyer Ministries—South Africa
P.O. Box 5
Cape Town 8000
South Africa
(27) 21-701-1056

Joyce Meyer Ministries—Francophonie
29 avenue Maurice Chevalier
77330 Ozoir la Ferriere
France

Joyce Meyer Ministries—Germany
Postfach 761001
22060 Hamburg
Germany
+49 (0)40 / 88 88 4 11 11

Joyce Meyer Ministries—Netherlands
Lorenzlaan 14
7002 HB Doetinchem
+31 657 555 9789

Joyce Meyer Ministries—Russia
P.O. Box 789
Moscow 101000
Russia
+7 (495) 727-14-68

OTHER BOOKS BY JOYCE MEYER

JOYCE MEYER SPANISH TITLES

Auténtica y única (Authentically, Uniquely You)
Belleza en lugar de cenizas (Beauty for Ashes)
Buena salud, buena vida (Good Health, Good Life)
Cambia tus palabras, cambia tu vida (Change Your Words, Change Your Life)
El campo de batalla de la mente (Battlefield of the Mind)
Cómo envejecer sin avejentarse (How to Age without Getting Old)
Como formar buenos habitos y romper malos habitos (Making Good Habits, Breaking Bad Habits)
La conexión de la mente (The Mind Connection)
Dios no está enojado contigo (God Is Not Mad at You)
La dosis de aprobación (The Approval Fix)
Efesios: Comentario biblico (Ephesians: Biblical Commentary)
Empezando tu día bien (Starting Your Day Right)
Hágalo con miedo (Do It Afraid)
Hazte un favor a ti mismo...perdona (Do Yourself a Favor...Forgive)
Madre segura de sí misma (The Confident Mom)
Momentos de quietud con Dios (Quiet Times with God Devotional)
Mujer segura de sí misma (The Confident Woman)
No se afane por nada (Be Anxious for Nothing)
Pensamientos de poder (Power Thoughts)
Sanidad para el alma de una mujer (Healing the Soul of a Woman)
Sanidad para el alma de una mujer, devocionario (Healing the Soul of a Woman Devotional)
Santiago: Comentario bíblico (James: Biblical Commentary)
Sobrecarga (Overload)*
Sus batallas son del Señor (Your Battles Belong to the Lord)
Termina bien tu día (Ending Your Day Right)
Tienes que atreverte (I Dare You)
Usted puede comenzar de nuevo (You Can Begin Again)
Viva amando su vida (Living a Life You Love)
Viva valientemente (Living Courageously)
Vive por encima de tus sentimientos (Living beyond Your Feelings)

* Study Guide available for this title

BOOKS BY DAVE MEYER

Life Lines